DISCARDED
BY
BERTHOUD COMMUNITY
LIBRARY DISTRICT

D0466251

Investigating Science

Why does light cast shadows?

Jacqui Bailey

A⁺

Smart Apple Media

Berthoud Public Library
Berthoud, Colorado

First published in 2005 by Franklin Watts
96 Leonard Street, London EC2A 4XD

Franklin Watts Australia
45-51 Huntley Street, Alexandria, NSW 2015

This edition published under license from Franklin Watts. All rights reserved. Copyright © 2005 Franklin Watts

Editor: Jennifer Schofield, **Design:** Rachel Hamdi/Holly Mann, **Picture researcher:** Diana Morris, **Photography:** Andy Crawford, unless otherwise acknowledged

Acknowledgements:
Frank Blackburn/Ecoscene: 14t. Stephen Coyne/Ecoscene: 27b. Branimir Gjetvaj/branimirphoto.ca/
Photographers Direct: 10t. Chinch Gryniewicz/Ecoscene: 29. Chris Fairclough: 11. Ray Moller: 4, 10b, 13.
Laura Sivell/Ecoscene: 28

With thanks to our models: Mia Hanlon, Ross Zavros, Nikisha Grant, Ammar Duffus, Robin Stevens

Published in the United States by Smart Apple Media
2140 Howard Drive West, North Mankato, Minnesota 56003

U.S. publication copyright © 2007 Smart Apple Media
International copyright reserved in all countries. No part of this book may be reproduced in any form without written permission from the publisher.
Printed in the United States of America

Library of Congress Cataloging-in-Publication Data

Bailey, Jacqui.
Why does light cast shadows? / by Jacqui Bailey.
p. cm. — (Investigating science)
ISBN-13 : 978-1-58340-927-5
Includes index.
1. Light—Juvenile literature. 2. Shades and shadows—Juvenile literature. I. Title.

QC360.B348 2006
535—dc22   2005052554

9 8 7 6 5 4 3 2 1

Contents

What is light?

Light lets us see things. Without light, we would not be able to see anything at all.

THINK about the differences between light and dark.

● In the daytime, it is light outside and things are easy to see.

● It is hard to see at night in the dark. We use electric lights to help us.

How well can you see without light?

You will need:

A blindfold (e.g. a pillowcase) ✔

A friend ✔

Some small "mystery" objects ✔

A large tin or a box with a lid ✔

What can you see in the dark?

① Sit on the floor. Ask your friend to tie the blindfold over your eyes. Make sure you cannot see anything.

2 Ask your friend to put the "mystery" objects inside the tin or box and close the lid.

3 Double-check that there is no light coming through the blindfold. Open the tin or box and take out the objects, one at a time. Can you see what they are? Try to figure out what they are by feeling them. Tell your friend what you think each "mystery" object is.

4 Slowly lift the blindfold. How far do you have to lift it before you can see if you were right?

Because . . .

You cannot see what the objects are when you are blindfolded because the blindfold has blocked out the light. Light lets us see. Seeing is one of our five **senses**. *When there is no light, we must use some of our other senses, such as touch or smell, to figure out what things are.*

How do we see?

We see when light gets inside our eyes.

THINK about how you see.

pupil

- When your eyelids are open, light enters your eyes through the dark hole in the middle, called the **pupil**.

- When your eyelids are closed, no light can enter the pupil, and you cannot see.

Does the amount of light make a difference in how well you see?

You will need:

A mirror ✔

A pencil and paper ✔

A darkened room ✔

A small alarm clock ✔

8

How does light change your eyes?

1 Look at your pupils in the mirror.

2 Make a drawing of your eyes to show how big the pupils are compared to the rest of your eye.

3 Sit in a dark room for three minutes—use the alarm clock to time yourself.

4 Go back into normal light and immediately look at your pupils again. Compare them with your drawing. Is there a difference? What happens to your pupils as you look in the mirror?

Because . . .

Your pupils are larger after being in the dark because they change size depending on how much light there is around you. When it is dark, they open up as wide as they can to let in as much light as possible. In very bright light, they become as small as they can to stop the bright light from damaging your eyes.

Bright as day

During the day, the **sun** gives us all the light we need.

⚠ Bright lights can hurt your eyes. The sun's light is the brightest light of all. Never look directly at the sun; doing so could make you blind.

THINK about the light from the sun.
• On a sunny day, things look bright and clear.
• When it is cloudy, everything looks duller, but we can still see.

How strong do you think the sun's light is?

You will need:
A pencil ✔
A sheet of paper ✔

How strong is sunlight?

① Go outside on a day when it is sunny but there are also clouds in the sky.

② Look around you. How does everything look when the sun is shining? Make a list, as shown here, and note how clearly you can see things. What do the colors look like? Do some things sparkle?

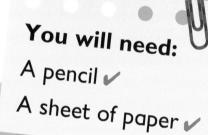

3 Wait for the sun to go behind a cloud. Now look around you again. What differences can you see? Write them down.

4 Look at the picture above. How do you think this picture would change if the sun went behind a cloud?

Because . . .

When there are clouds in the sky, the daylight is dim, and colors are less bright. This is because the clouds are blocking some of the sun's light. But clouds cannot block all of the sun's light. Sunlight is too strong.

The sun's light is the strongest type of light. It spreads for millions and millions of miles throughout space.

Lights at night

At nighttime, or in places where sunlight cannot reach, we use **artificial light sources**—things that give us light.

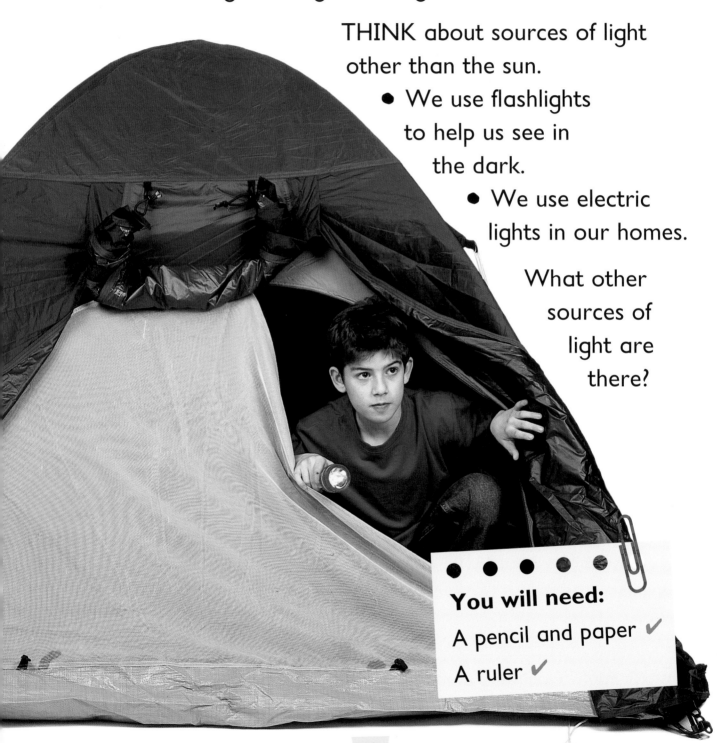

THINK about sources of light other than the sun.

- We use flashlights to help us see in the dark.
- We use electric lights in our homes.

What other sources of light are there?

You will need:

A pencil and paper ✔

A ruler ✔

How many light sources can you find?

1 Divide your piece of paper into three columns.

2 In the first column, list all of the things that give off light, both indoors and outdoors. For example: house lights, fires, candles, and computer screens.

3 In the second column, write down what makes each light source work. For example: electricity and fire. Ask an adult if you are not sure.

4 In the third column, rate each light source from 1 to 3 for its level of brightness: 1 = dazzling, 2 = easy to see by, 3 = hard to see by.

5 Which light sources are the brightest?

Because . . .

Some lights are brighter than others because they are more powerful. The brightest lights are usually electric lights. Light that comes from a burning candle or wood is weak and may not last very long.

*Some things that shine brightly are not light sources. They do not make their own light, but bounce—or **reflect**—light from elsewhere. The **moon** reflects light from the sun, for example. See pages 16–17.*

Traveling light

Light travels outward from its source in straight lines.

THINK about how you can see lines of light.

• A beam of light from a flashlight is straight—it does not curve or bend.

• In a forest, you can sometimes see lines, or beams, of sunlight shining through the branches of the trees.

Can you see how light travels?

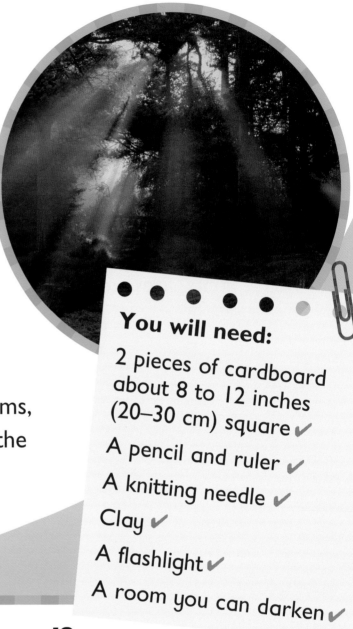

You will need:

2 pieces of cardboard about 8 to 12 inches (20–30 cm) square ✔

A pencil and ruler ✔

A knitting needle ✔

Clay ✔

A flashlight ✔

A room you can darken ✔

How does light travel?

1 Find the center of both squares of cardboard by drawing across from corner to corner, as shown.

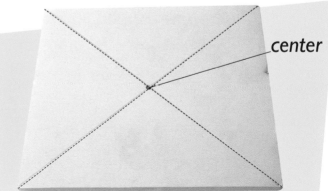

center

2 Use the knitting needle to make matching holes in the center of both squares. Line the squares up so that you can see through both holes. Prop them in position with clay.

3 Darken the room and shine the flashlight through both holes. Do you see a beam of light passing between them and through the hole in the second square? Adjust the squares until you do.

4 Now move one of the squares an inch (2.5 cm) to one side. What happens?

Because . . .

When you move one square sideways, the beam of light no longer shines through the second hole. This is because light cannot bend or curve to the side to shine through the hole.

Bouncing light

Most of the light we see is reflected, or bounced, off of the things around us.

THINK about how different things reflect light.
- A smooth, polished table looks shiny.
- A rough brick wall looks dull.

Which surface reflects the most light?

You will need:

Objects with different surfaces (e.g. a CD, a straw basket, cloth, a bowl, a block of wood, a mirror, a metal saucepan) ✔

A flashlight ✔

Which surfaces shine the most?

1. Spread your objects on the floor of a darkened room. Shine the flashlight on them one at a time.

2. Which objects shine the most? Do any of the objects shine when the flashlight is turned off?

Because . . .

Smooth, flat surfaces shine the most because light from the flashlight bounces off of them straight into your eyes. Light bounces off of rough surfaces too, but it is scattered by the bumps in the surface so they appear dull. None of the objects shine in the dark, because they do not make their own light.

Reflective surfaces change the direction of light. Try this experiment.

You will need:

A door ✔

A hand mirror ✔

Can you make light turn a corner?

1. Stand just behind an open door.

2. Hold a hand mirror out in front of you and angle it until you can see what is on the other side of the door.

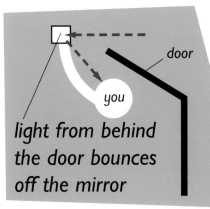

door

you

light from behind the door bounces off the mirror

Because . . .

You can see what is on the other side of the door because the light from that side hits the mirror and bounces off of it at an angle, into your eyes.

Blocking light

Light passes through some things but not through others.

THINK about what happens when light is blocked.

- Bricks block light so you cannot see through walls.

- Glass does not block light. It is used to make windows and doors.

What other materials block light?

You will need:

Scissors ✔

A shoe box ✔

A ruler ✔

A small toy ✔

A flashlight ✔

Tape ✔

A book ✔

Some test materials (e.g. pieces of paper, cloth, clear plastic, plastic wrap, aluminum foil, tissue paper) ✔

A pencil and paper ✔

Which materials block out light?

1. Ask an adult to cut a hole about six inches (15 cm) by four inches (10 cm) in the top of the shoe-box lid, and a square of about one inch (2.5 cm) in one side of the box.

(2) Put the toy inside the box and put the lid on.

(3) Position the end of the flashlight over the hole in the side and tape it securely to hold it in place. You may need to rest the flashlight on something, such as a book. Turn on the flashlight.

(4) Lay your test materials, one at a time, over the hole in the lid, completely covering it. What can you see? Make a record of the results.

Because . . .

*You can see the flashlight and toy clearly through some materials. This is because almost all of the light passes through these materials, from inside and outside the box. These materials are **transparent**.*

*Some materials let some light through them and block (reflect) the rest. You can see the flashlight glowing inside the box, but you cannot see the toy very clearly. These materials are **translucent**.*

*The other materials block all of the light, both from outside and inside the box. You cannot see inside the box at all. These materials are **opaque**.*

Making shadows

When an object blocks light, it makes a **shadow**.

THINK about how objects make shadows.

- Look under your bed. Is it dark there? The darkness is a shadow made by the bed.
- Turn on a desk lamp. Do the objects under the light have shadows?

How do objects make shadows?

You will need:

The shoe box and book from pages 18–19 ✔

A paintbrush and some black paint ✔

A large plastic comb ✔

Tape ✔

A flashlight ✔

How are shadows made?

1. Remove the lid, toy, and flashlight from the shoe box. Paint the inside of the box black.

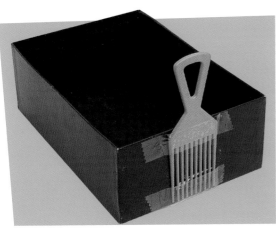

3 Position your flashlight on the book and shine it through the comb and the hole. What can you see?

2 Tape the plastic comb over the hole in the side of the box.

Because . . .

You see striped shadows in the box because the teeth of the comb block the flashlight. Light travels in straight lines—it cannot bend around the teeth to shine behind them.

Some shadows are stronger than others. A glass is transparent—it will make a shadow but the shadow is weak. Put something solid, such as a straw, inside the glass, and you will see its shadow through the glass. A mug is opaque. It blocks light, so its shadow is strong. If something is inside the mug, you cannot see its shadow through the mug.

Shadow shapes

An object's shadow is similar to the object's shape.

THINK about how
shadows look.
- The shadow a ball makes
is round like the ball.
- The shadow your hand
makes is shaped like your hand.

Can shadows change
their shape?

You will need:

An adult ✔

Scissors ✔

The same shoe box as before ✔

A plain white plastic bag
(e.g. a garbage bag) ✔

Tape ✔

A book ✔

A flashlight ✔

A chair ✔

Some friends ✔

A collection of small objects ✔

What shapes do shadows make?

1. Ask an adult to cut out the base of the shoe box, leaving a one-inch (3.5 cm) rim.

2. Cut a piece of plastic bag to cover the base of the box. Stretch the plastic over the base and tape it firmly around the sides. This is your screen.

3. Stand the box upright with the screen facing away from you. Put a book inside it to weigh it down.

4. Place the flashlight behind the screen so that it shines into the box. It may need to rest on something.

5. Ask your friends to sit in front of the screen. Darken the room. Put each object in front of the flashlight so that it makes a shadow on the screen.

6. Can your friends guess what it is? Move the object closer to the flashlight and then farther away. What happens to its shadow?

Because . . .

Shadows can play tricks on your eyes because all you see is a flat outline of the object. If the object is turned at an angle to the light, the shadow you see may be squashed or stretched out. If an object is close to the light source, its shadow is larger. If it is far away, its shadow is smaller.

Sun and shadow

Shadows happen outdoors, too.

THINK about when you can
see shadows outside.
- Are there shadows on
a cloudy day?
- Are there shadows
on a sunny day?

What kind of shadow does
sunlight make?

You will need:
A sunny day ✔
A friend ✔

How does the sun make shadows?

1 Go outside with a friend
on a sunny day. What
shadows do you see?

2 Stand in an open space
with your back to the sun.
Where is your shadow?

Because . . .

*The best shadows happen on clear, sunny days when the
sun's light shines directly on the ground. Any object that
stands between the sun and the ground forms a shadow
on the side opposite the sun.*

THINK about the size of your shadow.
Does it change during the day?

How do the sun's shadows change?

You will need:
A friend ✔
An open spot ✔
Chalk ✔

1. Stand outside in a sunny spot early in the morning. Ask a friend to make a chalk mark on the ground where your shadow ends.

2. Come back to the same spot at midday and mark your shadow again. Has it changed?

Because . . .

Your shadow is longer in the early morning because the sun is low in the sky. At midday, the sun is almost straight above you, and your shadow is much shorter. It is also pointing in a different direction. Why is that?

Shifting shadows

Shadows from sunlight point in different directions at different times of day.

THINK about how the sun's shadows change.
- Which side of your house is shaded in the morning?
- Which side is shaded in the evening? Have the shadows moved?

How do the sun's shadows move?

1. Start early in the morning.

2. Make a hole in the middle of the cardboard. Push the stick through the cardboard and into the ground so it is held in place.

You will need:
A sunny morning ✔
A sheet of cardboard ✔
A straight stick ✔
An open area of ground where your experiment will not be disturbed ✔
A ruler and a marker ✔
A clock ✔

3 Use the ruler and the marker to draw along the stick's shadow on the cardboard. Write the time at the end of the shadow. Be careful not to move the cardboard or the stick.

4 Come back every two hours. Mark where the shadow is each time and write down the time. How does the stick's shadow move during the day?

9:00 a.m.

Because . . .

Shadows always point away from the light source that is making them. The stick's shadow moved around the cardboard because the direction of the sun's light changed during the day.

Long ago, people used the movement of the sun's shadows to tell the time. Shadow clocks are called sundials.

Useful words

Artificial things are made by people—they do not exist naturally. For example, candles and electric lights would not exist if we did not make them.

Light sources are things that make light. The sun is a natural light source. Electric lamps, car lights, candles, and fire are all artificial light sources.

Natural light sources

There are other natural light sources as well as the sun. A few animals, such as glowworms and fireflies, make their own light. Lightning is a short but very powerful burst of natural light.

Opaque materials are things that we cannot see through at all. They reflect all of the light that falls on them. Stone and wood are opaque materials. Most of our clothes are opaque, too!

Pupils are the dark holes in the middle of the colored parts of our eyes. Light shines through our pupils onto the back of our eyes. Our brain then tells us what we are seeing.

Reflect is a word that means to bounce off. We are able to see things because light is bouncing off of them and into our eyes. Mirrors reflect light so well that we can see a perfect, reversed copy of ourselves when we look into them.

Senses allow us to find out what is happening around us. We have five senses—they are seeing, hearing, touching, tasting, and smelling.

Shadows are the dark areas that form behind objects when they block light.

The sun is a gigantic ball of glowing gas that gives out great amounts of light and heat. It is more than 100 times bigger than Earth and is about 93 million miles (150 million km) away. It takes eight minutes for light from the sun to reach Earth.

Translucent materials allow us to see light through them, but not much else. These materials let some light pass through them, but they reflect the rest. Tracing paper, sheer curtains, and frosted glass are translucent.

Transparent materials are things that we can see through clearly. Most of the light that falls on them passes through them. Glass and water are transparent.

Sundials

Long ago, people used sundials to tell the time. Sundials work using shadows cast by the sun's light. These shadows change during the day because Earth is turning. It takes 24 hours for Earth to make a complete turn.

The moon

The moon is a ball of rock that travels around Earth. We see it in the sky because the sun's light bounces off of it and shines down to Earth. Unlike the sun, the moon does not make any light of its own.

Index

Berthoud Public Library
Berthoud, Colorado